T0381408

YOGA BEST LIFE

5 Keys to Unlock Abundant Health, Wealth, and Happiness

ALICIA DUGAR STEPHENSON, ERYT200

AuthorHouse™
1663 Liberty Drive
Bloomington, IN 47403
www.authorhouse.com
Phone: 1 (800) 839-8640

Published by AuthorHouse 05/31/2019

ISBN: 978-1-7283-1379-5 (sc)
ISBN: 978-1-7283-1380-1 (e)

Library of Congress Control Number: 2019905910

Scripture quotations marked NIV are taken from the Holy Bible, New International Version®. NIV®. Copyright ©
1973, 1978, 1984 by International Bible Society. Used by permission of Zondervan. All rights reserved. [Biblica]

Print information available on the last page.

Any people depicted in stock imagery provided by Getty Images are models,
and such images are being used for illustrative purposes only.
Certain stock imagery © Getty Images.

This book is printed on acid-free paper.

YOGA BEST LIFE

5 Keys to Unlock Abundant Health, Wealth, and Happiness

By Alicia Dugar Stephenson, E-RYT 200

Namaste Beginner's Mind,

Here is the map! Use the 5 keys outlined in this book to unlock the best version of your life. Go at your own pace along this journey.

Advanced ways to use your map:

- *Begin again and again*

- *Recognize your current truth*

- *Deepen your breath*

- *Trust your inner wisdom*

- *Accept the abundance of the universe*

The yoga poses included are able to be modified to fit what your body needs. Your life-journey is unique from any other; therefore, you are magnificent!

Visit linktr.ee/afroyoga for additional support and connection opportunities

World Peace Through Inner Peace,

Alicia Dugar Stephenson, E-RYT200

LEGEND

INTRODUCTION

Problems

"Would you like to press charges, ma'am?"

…….. (silence)

"Ma'am, if you are not pressing charges, why are you here?"

His harsh tone brought my attention back from the daze.

Then I realized… I was right back in a police station, like the year prior. Doing the same damn thing; wishing I wasn't in an abusive relationship.

By that time, I had stopped speaking with all family and friends. When I talked with them, I felt judged by their disapproval of my lifestyle. I truly felt alone in the world. It was like my relationship was my only connection to love; a convoluted, mutilated, fleeting form of what I thought love was. Plus, none of it was my fault! I blamed everything and everyone else but me.

My work only allowed temporary relief. I focused on running a successful multi-million dollar business. I enjoyed working with several high energy employees and enthusiastic clients. But, after work, I'd get picked up in my **own** car by the same unemployed guy that I started to resent more each day.

Yoga became an outlet for me to let go of worry and regret. Each time I stepped on my yoga mat, I felt like a human being. Yoga afforded me an enjoyable hour of deep breaths without the stress of multitasking my responsibilities. I began to crave the high "after-yoga" feeling.

I loved being at the yoga studio so much that I began working there part-time. I felt compelled to enroll in yoga teacher training. During my teacher training, I learned self-transformation as the pathway for masterful teaching.

Who knew being a yoga teacher would make me a better person!

Because I developed a desire for a more-than-physical connection, I thought that I had finally found exactly what I needed in this restorative discipline.

I started teaching yoga to anyone who was willing to learn: inside the studio, out in nature, with veterans, elderly, and kids. Even though I practiced daily and took advanced yoga teacher trainings, I always felt like I was searching for something deeper.

As a new yoga teacher, there were still many blockages in my life. During yoga classes I could feel energy moving, but afterward, I was back at dreading getting picked up in my vehicle. Although I didn't have all the answers, previous breakthroughs reinforced and assured my chosen path.

Then I discovered wellness retreats! Better than a vacation, wellness retreats allow the seeker to step out of the daily hustle and into curated relaxation. Imagine a holistic experience where just making up your mind (and your money) to attend, changes the trajectory of your life. I quickly registered for the next one I could find. *Yoga + Vaca!!!* Some things just make sense!

SIGN ME UP!

Far, far away from the distracting everyday

Society disappears

Convoluted fog clears

From within, there is a way

For the first time ever

Peaceful cloister together

Uninterrupt silent solitude

Total connection

Clear intuition

I broke off contact in my dying relationship and hopped on a flight. Then something magical happened… my body relaxed. I genuinely enjoyed being me and meeting people again. I came home a changed woman. For the first time ever, I was happy to just be me, Alicia! I focused on being in love with myself daily. I practiced yoga, sang love songs to myself and said only nice things about me until I really did like myself.

Finally, I was free of the need for validation and approval from men to fill a void. I replaced that desperate energy with self-supported love. I realized that loving myself is the minimum requirement to truly appreciate the love that I have for others. Because of yoga and wellness practice, I have never been the same. I am forever grateful.

Nowadays, I pay it forward by sharing practices and learnings that have revolutionized my perceptions of this new season in my life. This positive alteration has reshaped me for the better.

Before you read anymore of this book, decide now if you are ready to change your own life. Only you have the power to change everything!

Preparatory Quiz

Practice listening to and trusting your intuition with these questions.

No negative self-talk or second-guessing allowed.

T | F I am 100% sure that I want to live the best version of my life.

T | F I am 100% sure of my need to embrace all parts of myself to have a happy life.

T | F I am 100% sure that I am ready start this work in my life now.

T | F I commit to be 100% honest and open with myself through this journey.

T | F I have lots of motivation to inspire my success with transforming my life for the better.

Once you answer T (true) to all the quest-ions you can trust that your quest to live well with yoga will be fruitful. If you answered F (false) to any prompt, consider that YOU are the only one who can make transformation happen towards your best life. Practice yoga to let go of *self-neglect* and *rewire your brain.*

Now, sign a commitment to yourself to experience breakthroughs for your highest good.

I,_____, commit to **work consistently** toward my Yoga Best Life!

Sign and date _____

Visit linktr.ee/afroyoga for support in your journey.

IDENTIFY

Do you wish to rise? Begin first by descending.
You plan a tower that will pierce the clouds? Lay first the foundation.

~Saint Augustine

I was nine when clumsy became my normal: I walked into walls, and dropped/ broke things everyday. Some time had passed since my parents' eventful divorce. My newly-single mother had moved me and my little sister to Southfield, Michigan. I was far away from the hugs of my dad, kisses from my Grammie, and the literal warmth of my Houston home. I felt awkward and disconnected in every way.

Fast forward to the summer after my freshman year in Baker College at Rice University in Houston, Texas *(GO OWLS!)*... I had moved from Southfield to Houston, and I now lived with my dad and step-mom.

I woke up INFLAMED and in PAIN. I swung my feet down from the bed and felt icy pins and needles shoot up my legs. I yelped so loud, my family heard me from the otherside of our Texas-sized house.

Ouch! Are my legs asleep?!

Several small excruciating steps later, I made it to the mirror. My vision was more blurry than usual, but there was no mistaking this! My cheeks, neck, and even my eyeballs were swollen beyond recognition.

WTF? Is that my face?!

Every. Thing. Hurt.

I struggled to understand that the days fatigue kept me in bed were connected to how my body hurt in places I didn't previously know were there. Six long months of weekly doctor visits passed. Specialists always requested at least 8 vials of blood, but were hesitant to diagnose me with anything.

I hate needles!

I lived on steroid packs during my rigourous second year studies at Rice. Everyday, I kept hoping I could just be normal again. The painful stress partially dissolved, but I still felt like I was in a war with my body. It was terrifying. I was fighting an opponent that I couldn't see and knew nothing about. I often wondered, "why is this happening to me?"

Luckily, I chose to double major in disciplines that I actually enjoyed. I found political science and French studies to be most interesting. I immersed myself in my studies.This allowed me a fulfilling distraction from my physical battle.

Foundation

The day I was officially diagnosed with Lupus was the happiest day I had experienced in 6 months.

Finally I had a name for my struggle! Knowing what was going on in my body allowed me to do something about it. I was able to research, talk to support groups, and begin a healthy lifestyle. I became preoccupied with taking care of myself, and I liked it!

My prescription for daily activity led me on a quest. I was seeking wellness, inner peace, and love. Finally, I found the solution in yoga.

Yoga, often translated as union, brings all parts of *self* together in awareness. Consider that knowing where we stand in life, gives us access to make the choices required to live freely. With yoga as your guide, there is no limit to what's possible.

Our bodies are wise vessels that allow us to experience this world. In every human body there are 7 main **chakras** [chaw-crah] or energy centers; they follow the length of the spine. Each chakra aligns with nerve clusters and encompasses endocrine glands. These electromagnetic locations in the body correspond with ancient eastern systems, modern scientific discoveries, and self study.

All your chakras work best when in sync with each other. When your chakra wheels are healthy, they spin easily (like disks). When balance is not aligned, it may affect how your chakras interact with the world. Examine each chakra separately to clearly see energy blockages in your life.

Start with the foundation or reality of your current situation. Become familiar with yourself through observation of your life now. Consistently turn awareness on yourself to prevent ignorance of your strengths and struggles. Allow your practice to be your teacher.

Energetic Quest-ions

Quest: adventure, investigation or journey
Ions: occur at a molecular level to achieve energetic favorability

Consider the following chakra-colored, energetically inspired inquiry points. A different color represents the energy wavelength emitted from each chakra. Shade in the areas according to the level of accord true for you. In other words, if the statement is halfway true for you, then shade half of the corresponding section.

Check out my exaggerated example.

PERFECT BALANCE

not a realistic example

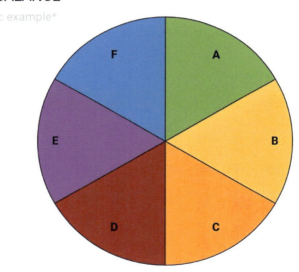

In this anti-example. This person sees that all inquiry points are 100% true and accurate for her life right now. If this were true for you in every example, chances are you already live Yoga Best Life.

I challenge you to get personal and real.
Trust your inner wisdom. If something is only half true, or not true at all, see your reality.

Red: Muladhara

[moo-la-dar-ah]

The Body, Survival, Grounding

A. I exercise often

B. I am healthy

C. I love myself

D. I feel safe in the world

E. I spend time in nature regularly

F. All my needs are met

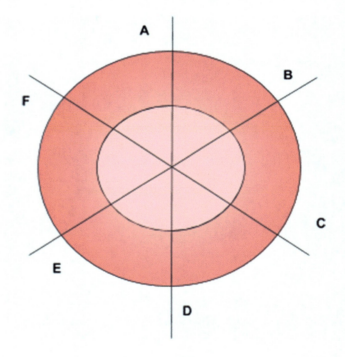

Location

Muladhara is referred to as the first chakra. It's name originates from the Sanskrit1 words; root (mula) and dhara (earth). Your root chakra is at the lowest point of your torso. Often in seated meditation, it is literally the place where you connect with the earth. In your body, your feet, legs and entire skeletal system act as the root of your being. In our world, Muladhara represents the earth element.

Significance

Your root chakra translates to the connection to earth (groundedness) and gravity. It's purpose is to create structure and promote stability. Muladhara is represented as red in color or dark brown, like the earth. When in optimal function, you may experience safety and stability within your body and environment. The human skeleton is a part of this solid energy.

Orange: Svadhistana

[Svah-dee-stah-nah]

Emotions, Sexuality, Change

A. I am flexible

B. I am affectionate toward others

C. I am satisfied with my sex life

D. I express emotion freely

E. I adapt easily in any situation

F. I embrace the flow of life

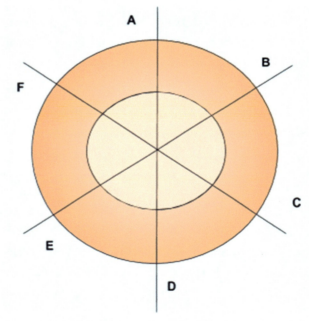

Sanskrit: an ancient language reported to have originated in India

Location

The second chakra encompasses the sacral area, between the navel and genitals. In Sanksrit, Svadhistana is often called the "seat of life". The sacral chakra is home to your reproductive organs, kidneys, and bladder. Your entire circulatory system flows with fluid energy. On earth Svadhistana is represented by the water element.

Significance

Your orange sacral chakra connects with pleasure, sexuality and emotions. It's purpose is to let go and let flow. Benefit from the sacral chakra: adapt to change within your body and environment with desire, pleasure, and procreation. When the sacral energy is closed, difficulties with reproduction, excretion, and the lower back may arise.

Yellow: Manipura

[mah-nee-poo-rrah]

Power, Fire, Will

A. I set and achieve goals

B. I feel powerful

C. I have healthy digestion

D. I enjoy being myself

E. I am energetic

F. I have high self-esteem

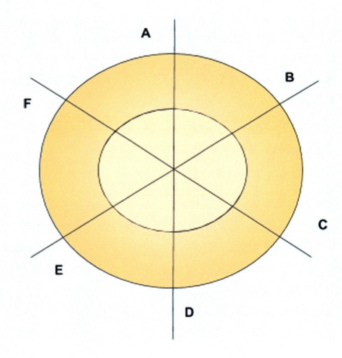

Location

Chakra three is the "lustrous gem", Manipura, in Sanskrit. The solar plexus chakra is located midway from heart and navel, around the digestive system, adrenal glands and pancreas. Your body's muscles directly correlate to this fire energy. Manipura relates to the earth element fire.

Significance

A strong connection to Solar Plexus may signify high self-esteem, a strong will and good digestion. When this yellow solar energy is open, you have the power and ability to take action in your life. This energy center may be off balance if you physically experience digestive difficulties, chronic fatigue, and hypertension. Energetic deficiency at this level may lead to powerlessness, stagnation of action, and low self-esteem.

Green: Anahata

[ah-nah-hah-tah]

Love, Balance, Acceptance

A. I live in peace

B. I love who I am

C. I make friends easily

D. I am optimistic

E. I feel inspired by life

F. I am well balanced

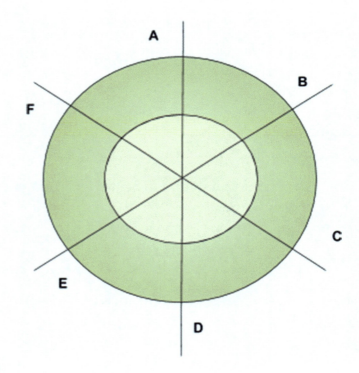

Location

Anahata in Sanskrit means "sound that is made without any two things striking". It represents a radiant energy center of peace and coexistence. Anahata is found in the heart (*middle*) of all seven major body energy centers. The heart chakra energy emanates through the heart, lungs, arms, and hands. Anahata directly relates to the air element in our world.

Significance

The fourth chakra is often represented as green in color. It balances the upper and lower energy centers. When in optimal state, your heart chakra vibrates with love and compassion. Difficulties at this energetic level may relate to abnormal blood pressure as well as disease in your heart and lungs.

Blue: Visuddha

[vee-shoo-dah]

Communication, Self Expression, Creativity

A. I communicate effectively

B. I enjoy expressing myself

C. I feel heard by others

D. I have integrity

E. I listen well

F. I always speak truth

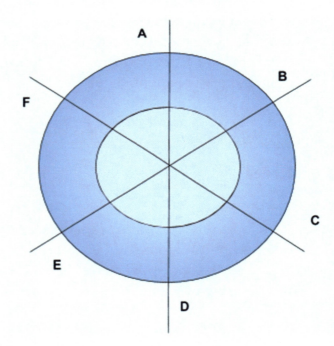

Location

The fifth chakra is throat chakra. It encircles the neck and shoulders; notably the thyroid and parathyroid. Visuddha, translated from Sanskrit as "essentially pure", manifests as the unseen element of space, also called the ether. This energetic plane governs sound in the world.

Significance

The bright blue throat chakra resonates in the world through sound and creative works. When functioning optimally, you communicate clearly and are understood well by your inner-self and others. Malfunction in the body's fifth energy level may reflect sore throat, stiff neck, hearing and (para)thyroid problems.

INDIGO: Anja

[ahn-hah]

Intuition, Perception, Visualization

A. I notice details in my environment

B. I have a vivid imagination

C. I have clear eyesight

D. I experience my dreams clearly

E. I visualize things often

F. I observe with intention

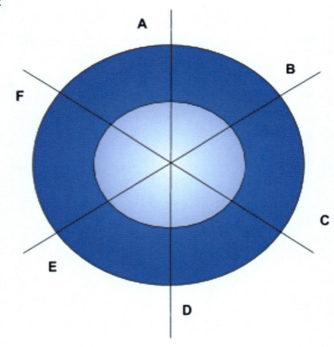

Location

    Your sixth chakra rests above eye level and is thus called the brow chakra. In Sanskrit, Anja, is translated to perceive and to command. The Carotid Plexus, at vertebra C1 and C2, correlates with the pineal gland and the eyes. It is interesting to note that this chakra is not in the torso, as many of the chakras are; it is found in your head. Anja corresponds to the earth element light.

Significance

    Indigo is associated with your sixth chakra. This energetic plane taps into sight and imagination. When it operates well you have the ability to receive information from your environment via your eyes, and manifest into reality a vision from your mind. Malfunction at this level may lead to headaches, nightmares and vision deficiencies.

Violet: Sahasrara

[sa-hah-srah-rah]

Understanding, Thought, Wisdom

A. I am aware of my thoughts

B. I love to learn

C. I meditate / pray / reflect

D. I am intellectual

E. I am spiritual

F. I am connected with the divine

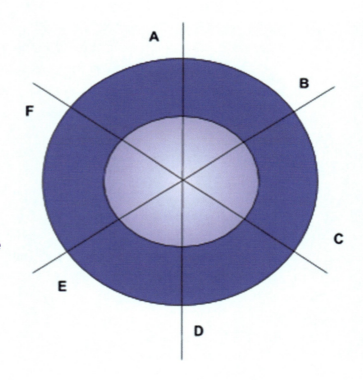

Location

The crown chakra refers to the cerebral area at the top of the head. In Sanskrit, Sahasrara, is the thousand fold seat of divine consciousness. The pituitary gland, brain and central nervous system are encircled by the energetic field of the seventh chakra. In the world, it represents the thought element.

Significance

The color representation is most often violet, and sometimes white (depending on the school of thought). Translated from Sanskrit to mean thousandfold, Sahasrara connects us to infinite intelligence. When healthy, the crown chakra allows understanding or knowing information. When it's blocked you may feel confused, depressed or bored.

You have just responded to energetic wavelength based, color-coded, thought provoking stimuli. Now, you may notice where you experienced the most energetic challenge, including: difficulty responding, feeling stuck or closed off, or skipping the section. Consider that challenge areas may offer the most potential for growth.

There is no requirement of perfection or filling in the circles completely at this time. This is a tool to know where you stand in the present moment, so that you may be equipped with awareness along your journey to live Yoga Best Life.

------------------ **Apply** ------------------

In your physical and non physical yoga practice...

Observe and identify what you feel and where you feel it. Avoid altering your practice. Instead, identify what is present in your body. Pay attention to where you feel energy. You might sense where energy feels blocked, tense, warm, open, etc.

Journal any insight from your chakras in asana (yoga poses), and reflection.

Namaste[2]

---

2 **Namaste:** a salutation passed down from ancient yogis as a way to acknowledge each other's inner light

Standing Wide Legged Forward Fold Pose

1. Start standing with arms and legs outstretched
2. Inhale, turn your toes inward toward each other
3. Exhale, fold at hips and use hands on legs to help press your crown toward earth
4. Inhale, imagine you could draw your breath to the base of your spine
5. Exhale, reach both ends of your spinal column away from each other

SHIFT

"Congratulations, you're self aware: now what?"
~ Frances McIntosh

My first vehicle was a motorcycle. A big ol' Honda...well actually, a cute lil' 250cc Honda Rebel. To me it was big! Big Freedom! I rode the open road on my open ride. I was wild and free as a bird... an Alicia bird. I felt giddy-ness vibrate through me each time the engine came alive. On rides, I'd see so many bikes and bikers. I happily exchanged many bike waves (yep, it's a thing). We waved at each other, and for an unspoken moment, we were cool and connected. There were no doors or passengers to distract from the world as I journeyed.

Some time after that, I finally followed the advice of others to "grow up" and drive a responsible person's car. I got a small silver two door sedan. When I drove this car, although I no longer got wet when it rained, I felt invisible and vulnerable on the road. I would frequently arrive to places on autopilot, without noticing or remembering details of the trip. I quickly identified that this was not the car for me.

To my benefit, I later traded my sedan for a red, four door Jeep Wrangler. That same exact day 10,000 other people in Houston also bought their own Wrangler...or at least, it seemed that way. Colorful, lifted, branded, tricked out, and even stock Jeeps caught my eye on every roadway. My arms were getting a little tired, but I would still lift my hand to wave at every Jeep I saw (yep, it's a thing too). I was sure there had not been this many Jeeps before. From where did all these Jeep people come? What had changed?

Drishti means focused gaze in yogic terms. The drastic physical, emotional, and energetic difference in my driving experience brought my attention to…well, my attention. Riding a motorcycle, I noticed the other bikers and vice versa. Getting a Jeep allowed me to shift from seeing practically none, to seeing them everywhere. Wherever your drishti goes, energy flows.

I appreciate the contrast in my rides. It took my exciting, then boring, then exciting vehicle ownership to shed light on my personal experience. Once I identified myself, I could then figure out what I did not want. My drishti led me to piece together what I did want: recognition, acknowledgment, community and positivity.

Yes!

Human senses take in information every moment from all input sources. We see, hear, taste, touch, and smell to connect with our physical world. It would over-tax our sensory input to notice, process, and respond to all potential stimuli. Even our eyeballs are designed with an area that is more clear than the entire view. Our awareness needs a focus to get the most benefit.

Challenge yourself to see the best parts of even the most difficult situations. As you take this amazing journey called life, you can make it the best one by shifting your awareness toward the deliciously sensational parts.

Energetic Gratitude Journal

Here's your chance to shift your drishti (without needing 3 different vehicles). Start with the prompts below to notice the energetic level of your gratitude. Pick one daily to focus on (in any order you like). Feel free to continue this practice daily for as long as you like.

Express yourself: free write, draw over the lines, or do whatever method you choose in this book. Use it as a path to process your journey. Think freely and trust your intuition. Avoid self judgement, self doubt, or second guessing.

This is your practice. Practice is not about being right. Practice is most effective when done over and over, then over again. This is only the beginning *(every time you begin)*. Repetition is the best method to mastery.

Check out my example from chakra 2.

I FEEL

Seen, Appreciated, and Loved.

*The love between myself and my husband **feel**s like warmth flowing freely from my chest and in to my body and out into the world. I **feel** that my positive energy is appreciated and well received in the community. During classes and talks I lead, I **feel** the room's energy shift toward my desired outcome (powerful; soft; calm; etc). I **feel** worthy and accepted when I wave at other cool Jeep people and they reciprocate. Smiles spread warmly across my face when I see people I connect with; I love to share happily satisfying smiles.*

I HAVE

_____

_____

_____

_____

_____

_____

I FEEL

_____

_____

_____

_____

_____

_____

I CAN

_____

_____

_____

_____

_____

_____

I LOVE

_____

_____

_____

_____

_____

_____

I SPEAK

_____

_____

_____

_____

_____

_____

_____

I SEE

_____

_____

_____

_____

_____

_____

_____

I KNOW

_____

_____

_____

_____

_____

_____

_____

Continue your grateful thoughts in your favorite journal or additional space in the back of this book. Once you shift your focus on the things you are grateful for, you may notice increased appreciation for your life.

----------------- **Apply** -----------------

In your physical and non physical yoga practice...

Notice the pleasant sensations. Shift your focus toward where and what you feel (ex. tingle at big toe; warmth in chest). Even in the most challenging postures, you may choose to focus on: the gratitude for the support from earth, the flow of energy in life, the pleasure you feel, the beat of your heart, the resonance of your voice, the clarity of your perception, and the wisdom you have gained.

Likewise, allow pain, discomfort, or "negative" energy to be an indicator as well. Each of these can provide insight as to where extra attention is required in your body and life. Avoid judgment of yourself or circumstance so that you may focus on healing back to homeostasis (your healthiest balance).

Journal: Any epiphanies, observations, and learnings that come up for you as you practice shifting your drishti.

Namaste

Crow Pose

1. Start standing with your toes and heels touching each other on the floor
2. Inhale, extend your arms and ribs up overhead
3. Exhale, bend your knees and fold at your hips to bring your hands down to the mat
4. Inhale, widen your knees to connect them with your triceps
5. Exhale, press your chest forward and bend your elbows back

(uplevel option: lift one or both feet up toward your hips)

☝ NOURISH

"Then the Lord God formed man of dust from the ground, and breathed into his nostrils the breath of life; and man became a living being."
~ Genesis 2:7, NIV

From the ceiling, the masks came down.

People started to panic. Many rushed to save others: children and those in need. Under pressure, they had forgotten crucial instructions given by the flight safety crew.

"Secure your oxygen mask before assisting others."

Similar scenarios replay over and over in the course of human history. Many of us may feel compelled to serve others, even to our own detriment. Our culture is of service outward: we take care of our family, our businesses, and our community. At the end of the day, we may have little energy left for our own nourishment. You can't help others if you have not first helped yourself. If your cup is empty, how can you pour into others?

Fill up your cup with practices that nourish you. Notice drastic improvements in your health, wealth and happiness. Nourishment is more than the water we drink and the food we eat. We are always consuming. Look around you right now, everything in your environment interacts with your body. Notice the colors, images, sounds, and energies in which you are immersed.

Breath is life force energy, called pranayama *[prah-na-yah-mah]* in Sanskrit. Prana is life force, the most necessary form of human nourishment. Yama is the manipulation, constraint or self-controlled action. Humans make entrance into this world with a deep breath. Our bodies inherently know how to breathe; on average, we take about 23 thousand breaths a day. Inmultiple religions, breath is noted for its major role in the beginning of humanity and the universe.

People benefit much from being in a community, but they can be alone for an entire lifetime. Eating food benefits people, but we can survive weeks without it. Drinking water replenishes cells, but we can live a few days without it. Breath cannot be withheld from the body for more than a few minutes without dire consequences. Even though we can't see breath (unless it's cold), we need it. Our breath connects the seen and the unseen parts of ourselves. Nourishment from breath is most important!

Discernment of the breath is a natural response when our head goes underwater. Even as an infant, the body knows to breathe only when we are not underwater. Mammals have an inherent breath discernment ability to direct energy in, to, and from the body. Often, we may find ourselves holding our breath when the stress of life has us feeling overwhelmed. On the flip side, we can notice slowed and relaxed breathing when we unwind during a yoga practice or a retreat. People may even remark that you have "breathed" into them if you exchange nourishingly instrumental and transformative energy with them.

Wisely choose where you send your energy.

Breath is mostly an involuntary bodily function. Pranayama, or intentional breath manipulation, is a deliberate action. Learn to recognize and utilize the supportive energy of your breath. This is the next component to living Yoga Best Life.

Energetic Pranayama

Practice the pranayama individually (per color) or all together. Journal your experiences, epiphanies and learnings.

Sit comfortably for pranayama practice in a chair or on the floor. Observe your breath as a way to become aware of any blockages perceived in your body. Close your eyes and visualize a rainbow directly overhead. This rainbow has energy that vibrates at different color wavelengths and it shines onto to you for your highest good.

Imagine a healing red colored light enter through your nostrils as you inhale fully. Draw the light all the way past throat and lungs, down to nourish the souls of your feet. Exhale out of your nose all feelings of unbalance as displaced black smoke. Allow the red light to linger and illuminate both your feet entirely. Inhale red light through your nose down to fill ankles, knees and hips. Exhale any negativity toward your legs as black smoke. Notice sensations from the healing red light that now fills your legs. Take a breath into the lowest most part of your torso, send root healing energy to the base of the spine. Let the breath out through your nose cleanse adrenals and large intestines of any fear. Now that your root chakra [Muladhara] is illuminated with healing red light and cleansed of stale black smoke, take a few deep breaths in and out to feel supported by the earth.

Imagine you can inhale an orange light through your nostrils and into your pelvic bowl. Exhale to release any blockages of energy as black smoke. Visualize a deep full breath of nourishing orange light entering in through your nose and down into your lungs. Use the orange light to transfer healing energy into your entire lymphatic system. Exhale the things that do not serve your body, like tension in your low belly. Take a slow and deeply gratifying breath in through your nose. Use your in-breath directed towards your reproductive organs, kidney, bladder, and low back. Energetically nurture this area as you imagine an orange light illuminating your entire reproductive organs, organs of excretion, and low back. Feel your breath and this orange light sustaining you. Continue the nourishing and releasing flow of breath in and out. As you breathe, observe the pleasurable sensations of your sacral chakra [Svadhistana].

Imagine you can inhale yellow light from the rainbow into the area around your navel, below your ribs. See how slow and expansive you can make your in-breath at the space near your floating ribs. Exhale by squeezing your navel in and up toward your spine. Inhale, actively send breath into your stomach. Allow the fiery yellow healing light to flow in and dissolve any digestive difficulties. Expel out of your nose what does not serve your optimal digestive health. Breathe in, expand outward through your side ribs to nourish to intensify your inner fire. Give off heat as your inner fire vaporizes any procrastination, fatigue and shame. Feel for the warmth of your solar chakra [Manipura]. Feed your inner power with breath as fuel.

Focus on the outward expansion of your upper ribs as you allow the green light from the rainbow to flow in through your nose. Use the outward flow of breath to assist the softening of tension in your chest and upper back. Consciously breathe into the space around your heart and lungs. Imagine the green light soaking your organs in healing energy. Let go of tension in shoulders as you breathe out. Animate your heart space with even more breath than before. Take an extra sip of breath to expand from your armpits. Release breath out through your nose until only peace and self-acceptance remain at your heart space. Now that your heart chakra [Anahata] is illuminated with healing green light, allow it to nourish your equilibrium (sense of balance).

Listen to the sound of your breath come in through your nose as the light bright blue part of the rainbow connects to your throat chakra. Notice the sound you give off as you release unnecessary tension from shoulders, mouth, neck and ears. Inhale. Notice the sensation of breath as it travels into all areas of your throat. Consciously vibrate as you exhale to feel the sensation of audible self-expression. Feel for the subtle healing of the blue light as you inhale into the innermost parts of your throat. Exhale to expel any vibrations not in integrity with your desired resonance. Allow the blue light to remain at your throat chakra [Vissudha].

Envision an indigo light get brighter in the rainbow above you. Inhale, visualize the light come down from the rainbow to enter at the place between, and slightly above your eyebrows. Observe the softening in this very spot as you exhale gently out of your nose. Breathe in the luminescence of the indigo from above. Observe with your mind's eye, imagine it lights up your eyes and the space behind your eyes. Exhale, soften the muscles along the center of your forehead and the sides of your eyes. Maintain ease in your third eye chakra [Anja] to positively impact your perception of self and the world.

Imagine the purple in the rainbow above you glow strong and shine down to the top of your skull. Inhale, lengthen your crown upward toward the purple light. Exhale, release any negative thought patterns that hold you back from yoga best life. Inhale, stretch your head up toward the rainbow; sit tall. Exhale, press down into feet for support from the lower chakras. Breathe in to fill your body with nourishment from low back to the crown of your head. Exhale to soften the top of your head, forehead and back of your skull. Tap into your highest level of physical energy connection. Inhale to feel an energetic expansion toward the areas all around your crown chakra [Sahasrara]. Exhale, imagine your "reach" spreads from your current location to cover the entire planet.

-------------- **Apply** --------------

In your physical and non physical yoga practice...

Take a deep breath before you say anything. You automatically exhale as you speak in life. Speaking out is similar to sending energy away from you; sending energy towards the reality you want to create in the world. Use your inhale as nourishment. Fill your cup before you pour into other people and things.

Start now. Take a deep breath in through your nose, expand your lungs to capacity with nourishment. Exhale as you say "I live my Yoga Best Life, now" *(say out loud or in your head)*.

During asana or other self-awareness activity, stay connected to your breath. Feel for continuous breath flowing in and out of your nose. Become aware of any changes in your breath: holding, quickening, uneven breathing, etc.

Journal: Any epiphanies, observations, and learnings that come up for you as you practice nourishing yourself with breath.

Namaste

Reverse Forearm Plank Pose

1. Start seated with legs in front
2. Inhale, place your forearms down with your fingers toward your legs
3. Exhale, spread open through your toes
4. Inhale, elongate your torso from your hips
5. Exhale, lower your crown as far back as you like

☝ SOVEREIGNTY

*Daring to set boundaries is about having the courage to love
ourselves even when we risk disappointing others.*
~Brené Brown

Our first date was set.

I was eager for my first ever tactical gun course. (*I am a proud Texan*).

Before the class, we met up to retrieve the needed ammunition. It had been a few months since I had seen him. I was excited. After we secured the rounds, we returned to the parking lot. He had never ridden in a Jeep before, so he decided (*on his own*) to walk to the passenger door and wait for me to unlock it.

I had not anticipated having any passengers, and the interior of the jeep appeared disheveled. I panicked.

I could tell he really wanted to ride with me. But, there was no way I was starting off our first ever date on the wrong foot with the situation in my vehicle.

I took a deep breath and told him "no". He laughed and tried to unlock the door.

I took a bigger breath than before, and put my foot down. I said, " *You invited me on this date, so you will drive.*"

Instantly, I freaked out a little. I had never set a strong boundary, or been sternly against doing something others wanted to do. I especially had never turned down a request from a guy I was romantically interested in.

Yikes!

For a moment, he did not say anything. Then I saw it in his eyes.

Respect.

I had given him no choice but to respect my boundary, and respect me. More so, I learned that it is okay to recognize my own sovereignty, and to defend it with a passion that demands respect.

TAPAS

Tapas refers to the passion generated from yoga practice. This passion burns away impurities, or things that do not serve your highest good. When you actively envision the sovereignty of your personal boundaries, tapas helps clarify the energy you need to live Yoga Best Life.

Boundaries are like having a border around your country that protects your sovereignty. Actors seeking to engage with you recognize your boundaries; they acknowledge your independence, they ask permission, and they govern themselves according to the "law of the land". Imagine a fence around your property. You get to decide who is allowed in, what they can bring, and the terms of their visits. You are the defender of your own sovereignty.

Personal boundaries may be less visually apparent than a wall, a border, or fence. However, people can use indicators of your personal boundaries and maintenance to determine how they may interact with you. Boundaries imply safety. In areas prone to fires, fire fighters may use a technique of burning a boundary line so that any approaching fire will not pass at the border. Boundaries are designed to keep things you want inside, and keep things that you don't want, outside. Your personal force field of protection defines what is yours and what belongs to others. Embrace the freedom of self-ownership with tapas!

Energetic Boundaries

Use the following images to determine your personal boundaries in each energetic plane. Inside the circle, write things that <u>you want</u> to keep or add. Outside of the circle, note things that <u>you</u> <u>do not allow</u> or <u>no longer want</u> within each boundary. Attract your ideal lifestyle by visualizing new things or removing old habitual comforts.

reference ✋Identify to review chakras

Check out my example: Throat Chakra- Vishuddha

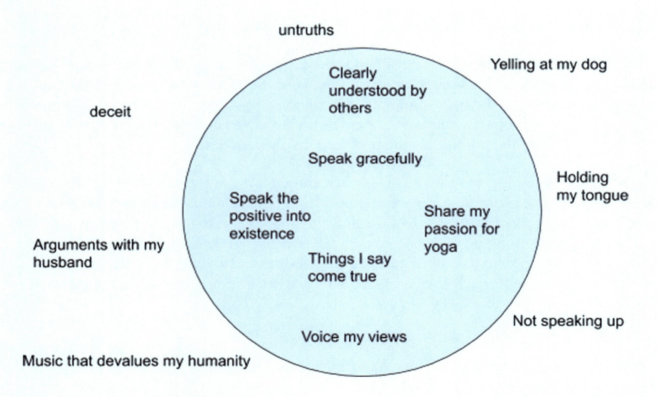

untruths

Yelling at my dog

deceit

Clearly understood by others

Speak gracefully

Holding my tongue

Speak the positive into existence

Share my passion for yoga

Arguments with my husband

Things I say come true

Voice my views

Not speaking up

Music that devalues my humanity

Earth Boundary

Inside (examples):
Self- Preservation
Healthy Protein

Outside (examples):
Fear
Unhealthy Protein

Water Boundary

Inside (examples):
Self- Gratification
Healthy Liquid

Outside (examples):
Guilt
Unhealthy Liquid

Fire Boundary

Inside (examples):
Self- Definition
Healthy Starches

Outside (examples):
Shame
Unhealthy Starches

Air Boundary

Inside (examples):
Self- Acceptance
  Healthy Vegetables

Outside (examples):
Grief
Unhealthy Vegetables

Sound Boundary

Inside (examples):

Self- Expression

Healthy Fruits

Outside (examples):

Lies

Unhealthy Words

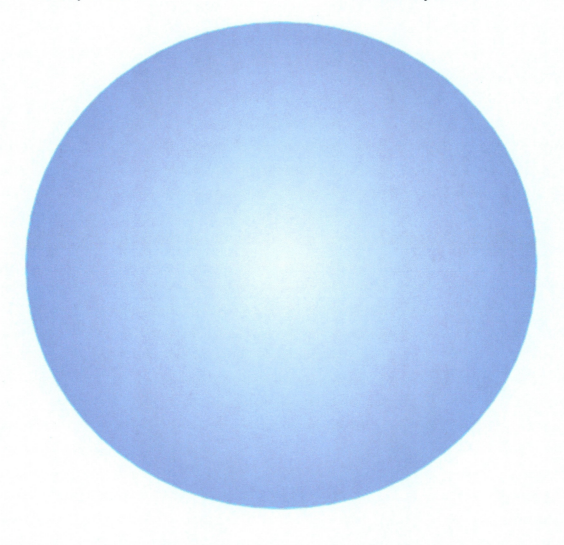

Light Boundary

Inside (examples):
Self- Reflection
Healthy Images

Outside (examples):
Illusion
Unhealthy Images

Thought Boundary

Inside (examples):
Self- Knowledge
Healthy Fasting

Outside (examples):
Attachment/ Obsession
Unhealthy Thoughts

------------------ **Apply** ------------------

In your physical and non physical yoga practice...

Now that you know and have set your boundaries, visualise them being concrete and impenetrable force fields. Your autonomy is infinite. Live your life in a way that you and others recognize the sovereignty with your personal energy.

During yoga asana practice, feel the boundary of your skin against the mat or the air. As you move and breathe, notice the ways your physical and non physical boundaries maintain the integrity you have with self.

Namaste

Plank Pose

1. Start with on all fours with wrists under shoulders
2. Inhale, spread your fingers away from each other
3. Exhale, extend your feet back until you're at the top of a push up
4. Inhale, widen your shoulders to press outward from the center of your chest
5. Exhale, press the earth away from you with your hands and feet

☝ BLISS

"Between stimulus and response there is a space.
In that space is our power to choose our response.
In our response lies our growth and our freedom."
~Viktor E. Franki

"I don't want to hit you. You're making me do this."

My disciplinary spankings as a child usually began with this line. When I got in trouble, I was made to explain why I had "earned" my spanking. After years of hearing these words from my parents, I internalized the the way I was disciplined. I believed my worthiness was tied to the perception of others. The impression that I deserved to be judged by others led me to adopt tendencies of unworthiness.

From adolescent years to adulthood, I craved positive recognition. When I didn't achieve at the highest possible level, I would assume I had done something to deserve persecution from others. I walked around trying to please others, because I assumed if they didn't like me, then I was at fault. I was always worried about what others were thinking of me.

In personal, professional and friendship relationships, I would go out of my way to please. When I felt in my life that someone might get upset with me, for any reason, I felt energetically obligated to do things I didn't want to do... like let people address me disrespectfully or shut the club down at 5am in Miami (*even though I wanted to stay in and not be out all night until the club closed*). **I would react; feeling unworthy and disconnected from my desire to feel freedom and happiness.**

Because I wanted every single person I ever met to indicate they liked me, I created blockages to my own natural flow. I would bite my tongue if I thought my words may be negatively viewed. Years of holding back things that I really wanted to say, led my throat chakra to be out of alignment. Until I learned how to claim my Yoga Best Life, life felt like a daily struggle. I had to learn to transform my own thoughts, speech and actions.

Everything in the universe operates with a natural flow of energy. This flow is powerful enough to grow and support life in all living things. Plants flourish in correlation to the energy of respective season, environment, and available nutrient. Life as we know it, grows, produces, and recycles according to natural regulation. The earth, the chakras, and even the tiniest cells spin and support life in alignment with energetic purpose.

Humans can greatly benefit by a connection to the natural flow of energy in the universe. On an individual level, it can be challenging to be in the flow. Different lifestyles can influence recognition of one's own inner energy. Humans tend to find a rhythm or muscle memory function that reinforces whatever patterns of thought, energy, and action are repeated. Unfortunately, even our unhealthy practices can be habits *(like addictions)*. This is why yoga, self-connection and awareness, can prove to be powerful when consistently practiced in all areas of life.

Each person is capable of choice in actions and reactions. This is especially true for the readers of this book. (Re)claim your connection to choice with a consistent yoga practice. Do not be mislead, however to believe that yoga is only the bending and stretching with breath that has become a trend in the 21st century. The practice of yoga allows flow to occur in all areas of life. You may choose to be in yoga during other activities, even writing *(like I am doing as I create this book)*. When you do, you can let go of your own desire to please others at your own expense. Yoga helps reconnection to your purpose, so that what you do serves your highest good: Yoga Best Life.

Energetic Flow Journal

The day I married my soulmate was the most emotional day of my life. I had prepared all the customary and unique aspects of our love celebration with my team, and it was finally here! The excitement was pounding in my chest, and I was feeling a giddIness that only true love can know.

That day, I was showered with love, well wishes and gifts. I was hugged, kissed and photographed by my guests so much that the beautiful venue felt warm and inviting. My husband spoke from his heart during our vows and a tear came down his face. *(Aww!)* *He kissed his bride.*

In these moments I felt warmth in my chest, tingles in my limbs and butterflies in my belly. As I wiped my husband's tear, his face felt warm and his gaze was locked with mine. I felt the moisture from his warm skin. The kiss! Sparks! I felt tingles when our lips touched. It was magical.

I chose to discern

> *+ that I am loved by my community*

> *+ I am emotionally connected to my husband, Karlton*

> *+ I am supported (his eyes never left mine in a room full of people)*

I will use this knowledge in the times

> *I don't feel as connected to my loved ones* *(when I am working or traveling)*

> *+ To remember how much they support my goals and dreams*

> *My husband and I have disagreements or challenging conversations*

> *+ As a guide for the support I desire to ALWAYS feel in my relationship*

I feel sad or lonely

   +   *As a reminder that I AM LOVED and cherished by those important to me*

Now it's your turn.

These sections correlate to each chakra; there are five questions per chakra. The first prompt is color coded and gives you the choice of "negative" or "positive". Pick whichever situation comes to your mind the quickest.

Breathe deeply through your nose and let your answers flow out of you. Be specific on what exact sensations you were aware of in each moment. Include as many facts as possible.

This exercise is designed to build on the self awareness you have gained through this book. Use the prompts, to identify your responses to different stimuli. Then you can shift your reactions *(if needed)*, so they reflect what you want in your life.

Example:

I always get mad when things don't go how I expect, and I always get red vision, yell, and cuss. I get to identify this, using tools learned from <u>chapter 1</u>. I consciously choose to shift my awareness using tools learned from <u>chapter 2</u>, so that I remember that I have choices. I will take a deep nourishing breath, like in <u>chapter 3</u>, as soon as I feel my vision change. Then, I reinforce the desires in my boundary from <u>chapter 4</u> with my actions. I wrote that I desire to promote peacefulness everywhere I go, so I will speak, breathe, and be peaceful.

> *HINT: Facts do not include things like…*
>   *(S)he made me mad or happy*
>   *Why? Because you choose to be happy or unhappy based on the facts present*

The most safe or unsafe day of my life was...

_____

_____

_____

_____

_____

_____

What moment(s) or fact(s) really stuck out to me that day?

_____

_____

_____

_____

_____

_____

_____

What bodily sensations did I experience before, during, and after these moments? Where in my body?

_____

_____

_____

_____

_____

_____

What meaning did I <u>choose</u> to assign to each moment?

_____

_____

_____

_____

_____

_____

How will I utilize the knowledge I have gained to live my best life?

_____

_____

_____

_____

_____

_____

_____

The most emotional day of my life was...

_____

_____

_____

_____

_____

_____

_____

What moment(s) or fact(s) really stuck out to me that day?

_____

_____

_____

_____

_____

_____

_____

What bodily sensations did I experience before, during, and after these moments? Where in my body?

_____

_____

_____

_____

_____

_____

_____

What meaning did I <u>choose</u> to assign to each moment?

_____

_____

_____

_____

_____

_____

How will I utilized the knowledge I have gained to live my best life?

_____

_____

_____

_____

_____

_____

_____

The most powerful or powerless day of my life was...

_____

_____

_____

_____

_____

_____

_____

What moment(s) or fact(s) really stuck out to me in that day?

_____

_____

_____

_____

_____

_____

_____

What bodily sensations did I experience before, during, and after these moments? Where in my body?

_____

_____

_____

_____

_____

_____

What meaning did I <u>choose</u> to assign to each moment?

_____

_____

_____

_____

_____

_____

_____

How will I utilize the knowledge I have gained to live my best life?

_____

_____

_____

_____

_____

_____

_____

The most or least peaceful day of my life was...

_____

_____

_____

_____

_____

_____

_____

What moment(s) or fact(s) really stuck out to me that day?

_____

_____

_____

_____

_____

_____

What bodily sensations did I experience before, during, and after these moments? Where in my body?

_____

_____

_____

_____

_____

_____

What meaning did I <u>choose</u> to assign to each moment?

_____

_____

_____

_____

_____

_____

How will I utilize the knowledge I have gained to live my best life?

_____

_____

_____

_____

_____

_____

_____

The day I expressed myself well or not well was...

_____

_____

_____

_____

_____

_____

What moment(s) or fact(s) really stuck out to me that day?

_____

_____

_____

_____

_____

_____

What bodily sensations did I experience before, during, and after these moments? Where in my body?

_____

_____

_____

_____

_____

_____

What meaning did I <u>choose</u> to assign to each moment?

_____

_____

_____

_____

_____

_____

How will I utilize the knowledge I have gained to live my best life?

_____

_____

_____

_____

_____

_____

The most clear or unclear day of my life was...

_____

_____

_____

_____

_____

_____

What moment(s) or fact(s) really stuck out to me that day?

_____

_____

_____

_____

_____

_____

What bodily sensations did I experience before, during, and after these moments? Where in my body?

_____

_____

_____

_____

_____

_____

hat meaning did I <u>choose</u> to assign to each moment?

_____

_____

_____

_____

_____

_____

_____

How will I utilize the knowledge I have gained to live my best life?

_____

_____

_____

_____

_____

_____

The day of most or least understanding was...

_____

_____

_____

_____

_____

_____

What moment(s) or fact(s) really stuck out to me that day?

_____

_____

_____

_____

_____

_____

What bodily sensations did I experience before, during, and after these moments? Where in my body?

_____

_____

_____

_____

_____

_____

_____

What meaning did I <u>choose</u> to assign to each moment?

_____

_____

_____

_____

_____

_____

How will I utilize the knowledge I have gained to live my best life?

_____

_____

_____

_____

_____

_____

_____

------------------ Apply ------------------

In your physical and non physical yoga practice...

Be aware of the moments when you feel sensational responses in your body. Notice when and where the sensations appear. AVOID SELF JUDGEMENT AND COMPARISON. If they do come, notice them and use the moment to reflect on yourself.

The poses that follow are intended to offer an energetic awareness. Some of the demonstrated poses may only be accessible with years of consistent practice. Follow the directions and use modification offerings.

Journal: any epiphanies, learnings and challenges

Namaste

Candy Cane Twist

1. Start standing
2. Inhale, reach up and engage your core
3. Exhale, fold chest forward and extend one heel back
4. Inhale, bend lifted leg and connect opposite hand
5. Exhale, place other hand on standing leg

☝ CELEBRATION

"Watch your thoughts; they become words. Watch your words; they become actions. Watch your actions; they become habit. Watch your habits; they become character. Watch your character; it becomes your destiny."
- Lao Tzu

Congratulations on the work you've done thus far! If you have completed the material from all previous chapters, you have quite possibly learned things about yourself you didn't know before. That's a huge win! Let go of the elusive idea of perfection and savor the experiential qualities of life.

This process is something you can repeat as much as needed. Start with successful identification of the areas in your life where you can improve your energetic vibrational frequency. Then shift your perspective towards gratitude in each chakra plane. Take nourishing deep breaths to bolster and uplift yourself from the inside out. Chose to reinforce what you allow and disallow in your individual autonomic existence. Finally, enjoy the natural flow of your present reality. Time to enjoy Yoga Best Life!

The Yoga Best Life journey is not designed to be short or quick. You are encouraged to stay the course and persevere through the challenges. This work is ongoing and forever rewarding. My teacher, Roger Rippy, always said, "the way you do one thing is the way you do everything." I feel like this is true, and to create Yoga Best Life, I say, "In everything, do yoga."

You may even choose to reinforce your alliance with each chakra by wearing the color that corresponds to its wavelength. For deeper connection to root chakra, wear red clothing, eat red foods, etc. It is imperative to: identify what is present in your life, shift your drishti towards gratitude, nourish your life with quality breath, choose and fuel your sovereignty, and flow with nature. All of these work together to form the components required to live Yoga Best Life.

Namaste

------------------ Apply ------------------

Root

During meditation and asana practice, observe every part of your body touching the ground. Focus on your foundation and connection with the earth.

Fluid

During meditation and asana feel the flow and rhythm of your heart. Focus on the sensations of pleasure as you move and breathe.

Power

In asana and meditation, connect to the feeling of fire within you. Monitor your energy output and resources to sustain your inner power.

Balance

In asana and meditation, love and accept yourself fully. Be aware of the pranayama (breath).

Sound

In asana and meditation, listen to the subtle vibrations that resonate from your inner or outer environment. Create space for silence following your daily practice. Start with 5 minutes, then increase time incrementally as needed.

Sight

Follow asana and meditation with visualization. Sit or lay in stillness with your eyes closed. Replay your practice as if you are watching yourself from outside of your physical body. See the images of your movement and notice any subtle visual observations.

Crown

Meditate immediately following asana practice. Allow thoughts to come and go freely, without limitations or labels. Experience connection to thoughts as they visit, then allow them to leave without attachment. Notice any thought patterns. Start with 10 minutes and increase time as needed.

Journal

"In yoga...the places where you have the most resistance are actually the places that are going to be the areas of greatest liberation." ~Rodney Yee

_____

_____

_____

_____

_____

_____

_____

_____

_____

_____

_____

_____

Acknowledgments

I am grateful to all in my life whom have helped me see myself and grow into who I am destined to be. Special thanks to my biggest fan and my favorite person!

Thank you to all the yoga teachers that impacted my journey, especially Albina and Roger Rippy, Dr. Kiva Davis and Heidi Lehto.

About the Author

Alicia Dugar Stephenson

Alicia's fascination with the transformative power of yoga originates from her lupus diagnosis in 2009. Thanks to yoga, she has transitioned into alternative medicine! Life changing healing led her to begin teaching and training other teachers to spread yoga far and wide. Yoga, facilitated by Alicia, creates radical shifts physically and energetically.

Alicia studied French and International Relations at Rice University. Her 200 hour yoga teacher training with Albina and Roger Rippy began her formal yoga training. She has grown into a conscious entrepreneur. She is the CEO of a high growth yoga company on a mission to Spread World Peace Through Inner Peace. Support the mission!

She has taught 2000+ classes including retreats, trainings and conferences. It's easy to tell that she loves her craft; she often teaches, studies, and practices yoga all over the world. Follow her @afroyoga on Instagram, do yoga, share yoga. Vi

About the Book:

You're smart, so why are you energetically not where you want to be in your life? Your life is pretty great as it is now, but you know you are destined for so much more. You've been looking for a sign to align your life with your purpose. Here it is!

Finally! A yoga resource that meets you where you are now! Learn to interact with your body's chakra system to strengthen your longest and most intimate relationship: the one with yourself. This book is designed for self-work by using the wisdom of your own body.

The Yoga Best Life journey is not designed to be short or quick. You are encouraged to stay the course and persevere through the challenges. This work is ongoing and forever rewarding. My teacher, Roger Rippy, always said, "the way you do one thing is the way you do everything." I feel like this is true, and to create Yoga Best Life, I say, "**In everything, do yoga**."

Get your favorite pen and begin reading. Discover what is holding you back from enjoying your life to your maximum potential. Complete the practices from each chapter to implement your learnings immediately. You already have the power within you, now is the time to use it.

Start your journey to achieve Yoga Best Life!

Referenced Works:

Judith, Anoedae. (2016). Wheels of Life, Second Edition. Minnesota, Llewellyn Publications.

Forrest, Ana. (2011). Fierce Medicine. New York: HarperCollins Publishers

Promotional Partners:

Clothes: YOGASKINZ.COM

Use 10% promotion code: YOGABESTLIFE

200Hour Yoga Teacher Training

$100 discount with promotion code: YOGABESTLIFE